black / *Maybe*

[An Afro Lyric]

Roberto Carlos Garcia

Willow Books
Detroit, Michigan

black / *Maybe:* An Afro Lyric

Copyright © 2018 by Roberto Carlos Garcia

Editor: Randall Horton
Cover art: Isabella Galarza, "Reproduction of Casta Painting, watercolors"
Cover design: Leonardo Zuñiga
Author photo: Ashley Johanna Garcia

ISBN 978-0-9992232-9-1
LCCN 2018935200

Willow Books, a Division of Aquarius Press
www.WillowLit.net

Printed in the United States of America

Contents

Acknowledgments

I am grateful to the editors of the following publications where these poems first appeared, sometimes in different versions.

5 AM Magazine: "Ars Poetica" and "Burn"

Poets/Artists Magazine: "Mamá Ana's Apartment in Washington Heights" and "Art imitating death"

Connotation Press: An Online Artifact: a version of "Back to School" and "Poem for Uncle Jaime"

Atticus Review: "Coward"

Adanna Literary Journal: a version of "The dead send dreams"

The Acentos Review: "The angry Black man," "Casta," and "Identity repair poem"

Gawker: A version of "black Maybe" titled "Hiding black behind the ears: On Dominicans, blackness, & Haiti"

Seven Scribes: A version of "Home [An Irrevocable Condition]"

The title of this manuscript is inspired by the title of the song "U, Black Maybe" written and performed by the artist Common on his album *Finding Forever.*

but what strange pride suddenly illuminates me!

—Aimé Césaire, *Notebook of A Return to the Native Land*

Las caras lindas de mi gente negra
son un desfile de melaza en flor
que cuando pasa frente a mi se alegra
de su negrura, todo el corazón.

—Ismael Rivera, *Las Caras Lindas*

Calling black people
Calling all black people, man woman child
Wherever you are, calling you, urgent, come in
Black People, come in, wherever you are, urgent, calling
You, calling all black people
Calling all black people, come in, black people, come
on in.

—Amiri Baraka, "SOS"

"It can be said that while there are differences in processes of racialization throughout the African Diaspora, in terms of categories that are used to define people, there are similarities when we consider slavery and racialist thinking...This positionality links people of African descent historically and contemporaneously, mapping a shared historical experience of slavery, systems of inequality, and relationships where racialized identity were created and recreated."

—Kimberly Eison Simmons, "Navigating the Racial Terrain: Blackness and Mixedness in the United States and the Dominican Republic"

"...the awareness of being black, the simple acknowledgment of a fact which implies the acceptance of it, a taking charge of one's destiny as a black man [person], of one's history and culture."

—Aimé Césaire on *Négritude*

Home [An Irrevocable Condition]

I remember the streets. I remember the cracked and crooked sidewalks forming patterns like neurons. I've seen life through these patterns, made new forms, retreaded old ones, and used them all the time like stencils. Concrete is my sounding board, my advisor, and hardship my silent navigator. *No matter where you go there you are.*

[Harlem / Washington Heights / Bronx NYC/ Elizabeth NJ]

*

I live in the suburbs now. "The place" my friend says, "where married people go to die." Yet I remember the two-family homes in my hood, leaning like they partied too hard—paint chipped front doors the corners rat-chewed, rusted hinges on rotting wood, and big shiny new locks like the gold Jesus pieces on the hustlers parked out front. The housing projects a never ending parade of bricks—warm and cozy in the winter, warm and cozy in the summer, and every season in between. Our faces began to resemble the bricks.

I remember the rooming house I shared with two crackheads and how they'd roller-skate uphill all day long. The two sisters who looked nothing alike, one of them had a baby, and when we got rowdy they'd become silent and invisible. The sisters shared the attic apartment with a haughty Argentine the crackheads were coaching-up from cocaine to crack. And the pervert on the first floor with his "nieces." And the landlord and his three daughters and two sons, the oldest barely nine years old, and his wife back in the motherland crying and sweating it out on Deportation Avenue. Nine year olds do knock on the doors of strange and addled men, and demand the rent. And rivers of malt liquor, blood, rum, and tears cut right through that house.

[Euphrates / Tigris / Pishon / Gihon]

**

I live in the suburbs now. I practice a new kind of survival—of symmetrical lawns, and they must be green, greener than the next and the next after that. And perfect. "Listen, why don't you use my guy?" Because "Everyone on this street uses him." I shrug. The patches of barren dirt and no grass are my answer to all of this. A giant clock ticks here all the time. We kneel and worship the clock. We rise from bed, eat, go to work, eat, come home, eat, do the kid things, sleep, and do the same thing again the next day. The clock is a demanding god. He wants it done the same way every day. Here the neighbors say, "Be smart. Vote for Romney," or "You can't trust those people. They're terrorists, all of them," and sprinkled in between, "How's it going?"

This isn't the violence I'm used to. I live in the suburbs now, *myself, split open, unable to speak, in exile from myself.*

One day the bricks came out my pocket. You see, sometimes neighbors write litanies and actually believe you want to hear them. And on my small patch of miserable lawn, the one asymmetrical thing in the middle of all these perfectly manicured squares surrounded by driveways and BMW's, shaded by oak, chestnut, gum, and pine trees, the pattern of the concrete emerged.

"You know," he started, "you should repave that sidewalk," then "and that siding could be power washed." After that, "You think you got enough garbage cans in your yard?" And, "Around here we usually only keep two." And, "This ain't the hood, you know?" And, "You should be careful with all that sun you're getting. You're starting to look like Obama." He reared back for another one and I jumped in on the beat, the one in my head. *What you eat don't make me shit.*

[Hood / Ratchet / Ghetto / Real]

***

I remember my grandmother's mop stick. To play stickball I'd use my grandmother's mop stick. To play fight on Saturdays, after the Kung-Fu double feature, I'd use my grandmother's mop stick. I used a steak knife to cut it in three pieces and with a shoelace from my sneakers and some duct tape made a three section staff. I was the man on the block like *huh, allow me to demonstrate the skill of Shaolin!* It was worth the ass whooping my grandmother gave me.

I remember my first full time job—six bucks an hour under the table. I stopped drinking Old English 800 Malt. I still bought my food from the chicken shack. Commercial streets consisted of Korean owned stores that sold imitation name brands, chicken shacks owned by Middle Eastern-ers, the occasional pizzeria or Chinese restaurant, and small liquor stores. On payday I walked down the long streets and bought twenty-two ounce German beers, then hit the chicken shack for a huge beef rib slathered in barbecue sauce, a double cheeseburger, and a deep fried chicken breast. Then I'd move along the stained, garbage riddled streets to my hole in the wall, *the working man's jackpot.* And when the beer ran out I ran to the bodega, and I can still hear merengue, bachata, salsa, and love ballads played over the sound of the deli meat slicer.

Night was the hook. The half dead street lamps created more

darkness. And from the pitch-black side streets, the sudden alleyways, and idling cars, violence exploded. Yes, I was afraid, but also alive. I got snuck [see: punched in the face unexpectedly] a few times. I regrouped with my posse and came back [see: large group and "Now what, bish?"].

But the day was just as capricious. I remember a drug deal gone bad, in broad daylight, my friend "R" the drug dealer got stabbed, and the posse chased after the crack fiend. I remember my friend Felix, blocks away, and fate guiding him to our turmoil, and Felix rounded the corner. A corner we'd turned thousands of times be it day or night. A corner occupied by drunks from morning to evening and Monday thru Sunday, beautiful women in mini dresses on Friday and Saturday nights jumping quickly in and out of cars, and young hustlers in loud cars blowing kisses and hooting with no concept of time. Felix rounded that corner — his eyes always on the lookout for us — saw us in the background and the hate in our eyes — and the object of that hate in the foreground, the crackhead. And there was no time, no way to measure the brevity of that breath, he tried to help us, to stop that man, but there was no time. And the crackhead shanked him, and took him. This is the violence nobody was used to, but we learned to expect it. I never lived here. I survived here.

[Mind / Body / Soul / Dust]

****

I live in the suburbs now. This is not survival — here it is idyll. Here there are toy lightsabers, Sony PlayStations, Nintendo Wii U's, Blu-ray players, flat screen televisions, iPads, iPhones, Mac book pro's, and home alarm systems. Here there are baseball gloves, bats, cleats, basketballs, and the courts are pristine, and the rims have nets. Here there is Lacrosse. Food spoils in refrigerators. And the streets here tell me nothing. Residents say the same things: "they're quiet, good people, mind their business, house always looks so nice." You can look but you won't *see* anyone. We're all pronouns without antecedents here. Every house is quiet, neat, and unassuming. My grandmother taught me to fear what I can't see.

I live in the suburbs now. I worked hard for this, strove for this, yes sir'd, no mam'd, and overtime'd for this. And I forget home for this — from time to time. And home is nothing to write love songs about, there is no romance, only the memory of hunger, adrenaline, pain, the growl of the wolves, and the cries of the meek.

[Residential / Nice / Separate / Single-family]

Mamá Ana's flat nose

Mamá,
if we *are* part Spanish gypsy,
            part Taino Indian,

why is your nose flat
like Celia Cruz?

Why's your hair deep waves
like Caribbean Sea,
skin never-before-seen cinnamon?
Why do I look like black Chinaman?

> *Mamá Pastora was Castilian gypsy, hair yellow*
> *Like piss from a rum hangover,*
> *Eyes blue like gunpowder flashing, skin white*
> *Like bones in the grave*
>
> *Papa Africa—Jose Maria, had hair tight*
> *As hide stretched over a drum,*
> *Lips full like the bellies of slave ships, skin Black*
> *Like bones in the grave*
>
> *My flat nose comes from deep inside them,*
> *Our skin, nose & hair an antenna*
> *To both ancestors,*
> *Beyond the grave*

We're not black, we're tan   Now callate!

Back to school

Plantains melted
onions & cheese
into the small sea of olive oil & salt
on my plate & after the meal,
after the glass of cold tamarind juice,
a nap in the shade, the smell
of palm soaked air,
sweet river water baptisms
I dreamt of Brenda Vazquez
& her Castilian slants,
Jessica Alba skin,
her high school sized ass in the fifth grade,
& I dreamt of going back to school,
sharing Dominican slang with her,
Popola, Aficiao, Coñaso —
I didn't want to vacation there at first
Mamá Ana warned me:
AVOID THE SUN YOU ARE TOO BLACK ALREADY
But the sun taught me I belonged,
it loved me blacker, stronger
I went back to school
& sought Brenda Vazquez,
walked up to her & she said:
Hay que Negro, tu pareces un puro Negro!
& my friends on the playground froze
then laughed & repeated:
El Negro, el Negro, el Negro!
Damn, why did I feel so bad,
why have I been sitting barefoot
on this small patch of schoolyard grass
ever since?

Back to school (*the B side*)

You ain't Black You Spanish
You Goya bean eatin'
Porteereecan

> *I ain't Puerto Rican*

You ain't Black You
think you Black but you ain't,
you Spanish

> *I guess you English*

Whatchusay? Crazy Spanish boy,
you dark, a little bit
See me? Black

> *Mm-hmm, you English too*

I know nothin' 'bout no England

> *My grandpappy's massa was from Spain*
> *Your grandpappy's massa was from England*
> *So who Spanish?*
> *Who English?*

A sense that something's happened

Then white snow began to fall
White snow so alluring, so ordered,

dressed trees in the less mundane,
made the paths mysterious

like life lines on a palm
Then someone keyed my car:

Fuck you in white against the navy blue,
keyed *Fuck you*—hid it in white snow,

we were surprised
Most of the white poets, like snow,

had floated into town together,
just them together, like high school,

like undergrad, like work,
the rest of us withdrew to the dorms,

drank wine, danced, a woman kissed me kindness,
I, grateful, tried to forget hate, we all wondered what to think

My professor asked me: *Do you think your car was keyed
because you're black?* I couldn't know for sure

We sensed something had happened
White snow returned—unyielding

Identity repair poem

(after Thomas Sayers Ellis)

NÉGRO

Négrito lindo (pretty)
Négrito chulo (smooth)
Querido négro (beloved)
Maldito négro (damn!)

SUGARCANE

Yeah, we go back
like sun & sweat
crack of the whip
greed & pain,
a trip across a cold salty ocean

AFRO-LATINO

Pedro Martinez
Jheri curls
Mongo Santamaria
Drums Drums Drums
Rum   Rum   Rum

LATINO (BLACK HISPANIC) CHECK HERE
LATINO (WHITE HISPANIC) CHECK HERE

I mean *soy negro,*
not Af-Am,
but I'm black
Verdad?

Mamá Ana's funny money

Mamá Ana said take
these purple, blue & green
pieces of New Deal bones
& go buy milk

I walked down the street clenching—
purple money?
Hidden in my fist
so no one could see

Crossing the street I almost got crushed
flat by a yellow cab but an old man
snatched me up
saved me
chastised me

You be careful, we don't accept
food stamps here!
You coulda been killed!
Watch where you crossin'!
Don't you know?
We don't accept food stamps here!

I ran to the store, saw
my neighbor leaving, she said:
Hi baby we don't accept food stamps here
I'll see you later, come by for cookies

I grabbed the milk, put it on the counter,
passed paper shame to the cashier,
squeezed my eyes shut

Coward

Words are harder to dodge
than his left hook would be
Hit me, come on pussy, hit me!
Players at the court's other end
stop dribbling, form a ring
around us   I feel them throb,
hear the hiss of frenzy beg
for blood How easily an elbow
fractures, when you straighten
the arm by the wrist & apply
pressure to leathery flesh
protecting bone   He leans,
shoves me with upturned
palms I wonder if he knows
eyeballs are softer than eggshells
That a finger jab could make
my face the last image
he'll remember for months
Hit me! What are you a coward? You scared?
I whisper it & almost believe
no one hears but they do
& all go quiet
"Yes, I'm afraid—I'm afraid"
The moment I decide
to suffer or to cause suffering
is quick I turn my head as he
connects, soften the blow
When I see my face in the fear on his
& the weight of my knees push
down on his biceps & I cup his face
with my fingertips like it's some   thing
I've created & the spit is gone
from my mouth, I am afraid

The day a poet I looked-up-to *clowned* me

He shook my hand so violently
I thought he'd shake me off
the map
I just finished saying my last name
when he smiled real big
& nudged me aside
He went to a group of black
students & introduced himself,
I stared at my outstretched hand,
darker than a paper-bag
& lighter than mulch
Oh, you're not Black black?
& I'm cast off
aboard my great-great
grand-pappy's Middle-Passage,
his slaver to
the blue-skied,
salt sea air of Caribbean cane-fields
Same all-inclusive package
as our cousins in Virginia
But in this day we are changed,
I am the space left in the wake
of the juke move
he performed to negate me
My blackness & me
shaking hands with the air

Chorus

Mamá Ana:

Ay no, pero

Isn't poetry about roses are red & violets are blue?

Write about *Quisqueya,* about
our Spanish heritage

No sufrás, hijo.

James Baldwin: A child cannot afford to be
fooled

Casta

Conquistador	Español	Peninsular	Europeo
Colonized	Amerindian	Indio	Americano
Stolen	Slave	Negro	Africano

Español	Colony	Criollo	Colonial
Indio	Español	Mestizo	Rape
Español	Mestizo	Castizo	Pass

Español	Maafa	Colony	Slavery
Africano	Español	Mulato	Rape
Español	Mulato	Morisco	Pass

And	It	Goes	On

Español	Morisco	Chino
Chino	Indio	Salta Atras
Salta Atras	Mulato	Lobo

Lobo	Chino	Gibaro
Gibaro	Mulato	Albarazado
Albarazado	Negro	Canbujo

Canbujo	Indio	Sanbaigo
Sanbaigo	Lobo	Calpamulato
Calpamulato	Canbujo	Tente en el aire

Tente en el aire	Mulato	No te entiendo
No te entiendo	Indio	Torna atraz

And	It	Goes	On

Terceron	1/3	Negro

Quadroon	1/4	Negro	
Quinteroon	1/5	Negro	
Hexadecaroon	1/6	Negro	
Octoroon	1/8	Negro	
Mustee	1/8	Negro	
Mustefino	1/16	Negro	
Griffe	3/4	Negro	
Cafuzo	3/4	Negro	
And	It	Goes	On
Trigueño	Trigueñito	Cimarron	
Rojizo	Moreno	Morenito	
Quemao	Quemaito	Prieto	
Indio	Indiecito	Creole	
Claro	Clarito	Blanco	
Oscuro	Oscurito	Negro	
Fair	Lightskin	High Yellow	
Redbone	Olive	Midtone	
Brown	Dark Brown	Black	
And	It	Goes	On
White (Not Hispanic/Latino)	Black (Not Hispanic Latino)	Native American	
White (Hispanic/ Latino)	Black (Hispanic/ Latino)	Asian (Not Hispanic/Latino)	
Asian (Hispanic/ Latino)	Two or More Races:	(Not Hispanic Latino)	

Chorus

Miguel Piñero:

he said (dips his cigarette)
 he never saw the cause
 but he heard
 the cause

& the Cause was in front of him

        & the Cause was in his skin

                & the Cause was in his speech

                    & the Cause was in his blood

seekin' the Cause

while the Cause was dyin' seekin' him   (gestures with cigarette hand,
keeping time with a silent beat)

The Lie

First time we heard the lie I was a little boy   Mrs. Hess, the red-haired landlady, took advantage of any opportunity to ask my grandmother: *Where's the boy's father?* & *You're his grandmother Where's his grandfather?* & *Why don't you people ever stay married?* & *My tax dollars support broken homes like yours with welfare*   Then she'd ask for the rent   My grandmother, tongue unable to lash back, unwilling to do the Tango called English   My grandmother, at a sewing machine eight hours a day, bartending slobs four hours a night, couldn't tell Mrs. Hess where to take herself, my grandmother let Mrs. Hess's tax dollars be praised, she prayed for my dead fathers, poor Mrs. Hess believed the lie & the lie has dogged all my days

Mamá Ana's apartment in Washington Heights

Clang of the police-lock supporting
the door bid us welcome
She'd step just outside it,
the wall behind spared little room
I was stunned
at how leathery & silver she was,
                how compact

We entered the short hallway,
a closet in the middle, door ajar,
too cramped to hang coats
The living room was
the dining room, a film of odorless
        grease cuddled each piece of furniture

Clear plastic over loveseat, sofa,
& arm-chair Oversized sewing machine
by the oversized window
& outside, a fire-escape, where
I drank *café con leche* from a tin cup,
buttered *Yeya* crackers,
        her eyes on me, *come mijo*

We watched movies late night, she talked
through the good parts & nodded off mid-way,
sometimes I'd sneak into her bed,
rats killed time on the kitchen sink,
she'd say, *Lie still & you can stay*
I did & I slept to the echo of her breathing
        bouncing off the close walls

Burn

That winter we learned to play with fire
burning whatever we could find,
our warm breath against cold winds,
coaxing the sparks

Jeffrey, the Frick to my Frack, was afraid,
My daddy told me, we have no business,
as young black men, playing with matches
Even though you puertirican

The newspaper curled in blue flames,
twisted into white smoke,
I punched him, *I ain't puertirican!*
Besides, it's only paper

We lit whatever we could
We got caught & Mamá Ana told
the neighbors it was a misunderstanding
She beat me with a strap, in the shower, under
a steady stream of hot water

That summer the older boys were burning too
Cursing about cops, *lack of funds*, the power
of the Asiatic black man & how Jesus isn't white
One of them smashed the stain-glass windows
of our church, shouting the same things

Pastor responded with extra collection plates,
Those windows have stood for 60 years!
The congregation gossiped,
All I know is from what little I've seen,
Hagar & Ishmael are black

They were cast out too
Mama Ana whispered in my ear,
They're not in any stain-glass windows either

Bricks (*AKA the Housing Projects*)

Who made these fucking bricks?
Made from despair & fear
Behind these bricks I am hidden

We
are
hidden

Rhonda, she's homeless, she says,
Life is hard on the streets but the streets are free
They can't hide you and they can't hide from you
They have to look at you, even if they ignore you

We
are left
here

Behind these fucking bricks,
only ourselves to meet,

ourselves to beat,

only ourselves
to eat

Voodoo

Cuban Feast 2002, we boxed through
the masses wandering closed off streets Spitting

& sweating, in the heat of September
At the corner, drums galloped

like horses at speed, people chanted, olive
skinned Cuban girl, jet black hair & her ass

like spiritual epiphany worship danced the
badoom-barrap-barrap- barrap Calloused palms

beat hard on the skins, induced moans,
Somebody bought a bottle, dark rum,

we embraced the darkness & danced, danced
Afro-Cuban priestess, from nowhere, hit me

with a chicken-bone, turned my head to
cinder block What? I cried *People hatin' on*

you, envy's all over you! She chanted & pulsed
in time with drums & I drank rum, back she came,

eyes like handcuffs on my mind, *Spiritual cleansin',*
you need Agua Florida & white rose petals,

bathe in them, set your spirit free
Olorun & Obatala are with you!

I felt hands, dizziness stretched
me into darkness, into corners,

& the crowd came towards us
wanting, drums & rum

& olive skinned Cuban sacrifice
writhed to the rhythm, I was losing my body

& I cried I've got to go, I've got to go
& the priestess blew rum breath in my face,

shook her wrists & said, *You're gone!*

The dead send dreams

Mamá Ana arrived from the island
a few weeks before her mother would die,
urged by her to leave the deathbed
& come care for us

She died on my birthday
The phone ringing so early
it could only be bad news

I'd been dreaming
I was standing on a crowded sidewalk
with my little cousin Josh
I looked across a six-lane highway
at another crowded sidewalk

We attempted to cross
but Mamá Ana's mother,
screamed from the other side:
No, no cruzes!
& I grabbed Josh's arm

A week or two later
he'd be mauled by a Rottweiler

& survive

Poem for Uncle Jaimé

His big, soft hands had gripped the naked backsides
of the pueblo's many married women
Jaimé Garcia beguiled with blue green eyes—
he was a stone cold fucking machine
& a well mannered mama's boy too
The *viejas* called him gentleman & *bandido*,
he eased up & down the lane, giving kids candy money,
booze to beggars, he even drank Sambuca with the cops
Jaimé crept on your wife as she sat in the shade
drinking *limonáda*, & you, away, working
Pueblo husbands half-suspected the infidelities:
they met & played dominoes to study the facts
It became a club of sorts, each husband pretended:
No, not my wife, passed off fake smiles like hyenas—
the doubt buoyant as a motherfucker
Then *Piel Canela* came to town   *Piel Canela*
because she was burnt like sticky cinnamon,
hair & eyes black like shadows in midnight's bedroom
Her teeth flashed wicked   Jaimé passed her gate one day,
saw her bent over, gathering dry palm for a *fogata*—
to keep mosquitoes away   He spoke slick   She finished
his sentences   The fall was quick & the toucans stopped their songs,
the river ceased its dance, & the *viejas* prayed
with *agua florida* soaked rosary beads, & Jaimé barely made it
out of *Piel Canela's* bed before her husband came home
& imagine him, his wife naked in bed, asleep—not yet evening
The feathery hiss of gossip carried him off to the domino club, to rum
Hands smacked domino tables in bitterness: Kill Jaimé Garcia!
Piel Canela's husband said no, that would be too easy,
& pulled a slight hammer from his linen blazer,
a hammer like a child's toy made of wood & metal,
with this, he said, I'll get that bastard   At night's sharp edge
they found Jaimé stumbling drunk along the lane
They beat him, took off his clothes, beat him some more,
& *Piel Canela's* husband came up from behind, held the tiny hammer
high up like a testament, & brought it down hard like a judgment
behind Jaimé Garcia's ear   The cry, my God, the cry
After the convalescence, the wives, like roadside flowers, waiting
& *Piel Canela*, so bold she met him at the gate as nurses walked him in

She searched his eyes for the blue green wildness   Drool
dripped from his lips   He was a boy, a dumb boy

Chorus

Miguel Piñero:

>   *and the Cause was dyin' seekin' him*

and the Cause was dyin' seekin' him

>   *and the Cause was dyin' seekin' him*

>   (chuckles, scratches himself)

Mamá Ana speaks on men in power

Será bueno mocharle
los juevos y
darcelas a un perro
con mucha hambre

It would be good to cut
their balls off
and feed them to
a very hungry dog

"A Dream Pimped": poem on the MLK Memorial in D.C.

I rebuke politicians   elephants & donkeys scheming   they
have   plots like onion's stink   making   the people   cry
a pied-piper's tune   democracy   pimped the
dream   to get votes   grow fat   keep office

I rebuke politicians   tap-dancing into   Dr. King's legacy   they
have at   his orations   push campaigns   rope a dope
a faith   pluck the divine speech   from Civil Rights &   pimp the
dream   I rebuke politicians   regurgitating & lapping up   Overcome

I rebuke idealists   like Mr. Drummond   thinking Arnold
might like   a fudge   brownie for his birthday
not because   he's turning eight   because it take *Diff'rent Strokes*   don't they
get race?   Dr. King's statue   made marble white   see that right
there?   & two blocks over   Einstein's statue is bronze
with all respect   to aesthetic   I rebuke I rebuke &
you   sometimes   too

Mine eyes seek   hope   my people's
eyes   see like   Superman's X-ray blues   we
have at fingertips Dr. King's Letters & Speeches, written,
seen & done   for justice & equality   if anyone asks   say
the man wanted   redistribution of wealth   not white granite
glory   show us   the economics &   don't pimp The Dream

Elegy Written for the N-word on behalf of the word Nigger by a Nigga

(it's cool man, chill)

1.

Fresh off the boat
Fresh off the plane
Fresh off the islands
& the hurricane rains

just got to the city
& already saying

My neega, my neega
Was good, my neega

Yeah, yeah man,
that's my neega

I be that neega

yeah

Got down with the hustles
Got down with the raps
Got a pair of tims
& a Yankees baseball cap

& you slap neega at the end
of all your sentences
& don't understand
the consequences

2.

X: Wasup my Nigga How you man
Y: Yo man
Z: Oh shit here we go
X: What
Y: Look man Don't call me nigga no more
X: What you talking about man
Z: Told you
Y: I know the truth about it now The hate
X: Nigga how long we known each other What you trying to say
Z: That's what I said B
Y: It's a racist word man Racists use it That cop that slapped me called
    me a nigger man She wanted to shoot me
Z: I can't be taking responsibility for history Nigga Or for white people
X: Fa real The fuck is wrong with you
Y: I'm woke to it now Can't let it go We gotta do better
X: Ok Malcolm Tito X I'm gonna say Nigga whenever I want
Z: I'm kinda insulted B I feel like you calling me a racist and shit
Y: The word is racist man
X: He is calling us racist B
Y: Y'all just don't get it man
X: Oh we get it You the one lost in the sauce
Y: Word How's that
X & Z: Cuz every nigga is a star   every nigga is a star   every nigga is a star

3.

I don't want to be forgotten
I want to be laid to rest

I'm not your intercultural
Metro-card or passport

My name does not prove
your bravery   I am not badge

I do not validate your story,
song, poem or friendships

No, I don't forgive killing
the oppressor   Don't care for *Taking it back*

Never believe no one's listening,
I am not prefix to

bulging crotch, lips, nose, style, ass, hair,
walk, talk, dancing, step or fetch,

I am not a brand or anecdote,
I am not endearment I am hate

I will never be forgotten I
am boogeyman Who said you can speak for me

"Puerto Rican GOP Delegate Interrupted on Convention Floor"

for Zoraida Fonalledas, Republican Committeewoman, Puerto Rico

Querida Zoraida,
que sueñes con
los angelitos,

bien puedas

You must give a speech & can't,
people only hear your accent

Aye que pesadilla!

In the crowd / Tea-party wags
wearing cowboy hats
won't stop shouting,
you can't hear what—
an alarm clock rings in
your Left ear,

the chairman bangs a gavel in
your Right ear, shouts
Order, order!

Cerrar ojitos & try to wake up,
No puedes, all the noise at once,
sounds like:

USA USA USA USA USA USA USA USA

Zoraida, do you still dream in Spanish?
I do, among my people

Pero esto no es un sueño
No son estas, tu jente?

Buenos dias Zoraida!
You are wide awake now

Speak the lingo

Latino:
person tracing
origins to
Central or South
America
or other
Spanish speaking
countries

Latin-oh! :
what
Spaniards
left behind,
reluctantly

LaTinO:
who knows?
Sounds better than
Hispanic,
which sounds too
much like Spick (No
Spick-ee Eenglish)

lAtInO:
source of confusion,
befuddlement
and anxiety
for whites, blacks
and others,
even latinos

LATino:
complex multi
-ethnic humans,
born from slavery,
exploitation
exploration
of
the New World

latINO:
what the world would be
if people marry,
reproduce,
without worry,
of race—

Chorus

Mamá Ana:

(long sigh) *Este mundo*

se esta

acabando

Irony

for Israeli Minister Eli Yishai (After the Israeli attacks on illegal African immigrants)

Burning building   Who set the fire   We   Eritrean   Sudanese Darfurians   are in it
My wife   Seven months pregnant   Is in it

Who said burn the building   Nazis or Jews / Jews or Janjaweed

Angry mobs   Police mobs   Spit on & beat   We   Eritrean   Sudanese   Darfurians
Women   Children   Bloodied   Condemned

Who urged the beatings   Nazis or Jews / Jews or Janjaweed

Here in the land of Milk and Honey
Here in The Land of Milk and Honey

We are pricked & bleed
We are poisoned & die

If we are like you in the rest, we will resemble you in that

Elegy for Nelson Mandela

For you heaven
will have no doors
only parades

will have no walls
no windows or roofs
people arm in arm

& living
a reverence
a kiss on the lips
living breath

will be an embrace
a *How in the world are you?*
intimate & innocent
& mercy a wild whirlpool

For you heaven,
a marquee in gold
a soundtrack:
blessed are they

a nine decade feast
Rolihlahla- "troublemaker"
blessed are the stubborn
who have a sense of fairness

of joyful tears
of humility

of constant dancing
of searing passion

For you heaven,
your mother's eyes
& you never look down

your father's hand
a pledge soaked in feather crowns
you stopped descending long ago

You won't see
black face white face
the enemy's death mask

the minstrel show
happying up oppression
they are portraying Mandela

Brother Madibi
on a bulging sleigh
no no no no no

you are not Kris Kringle
bearing gifts for peace
you were militant & ready

You won't see
chumps & fools, crying

your long line of enemies
I loved Mandela! I did!

Kissing your corpse's ass   with one lip
mumbling *Traitor,*   *Communist*, with the other

Art imitating death

Elegy for Israel Hernandez-Llach

1.

Sst. Sst. Sssssssssssssst
Clack clack   Clack
Ssssssssssssssst Sssssssst
Clack   Clack Clackalackalack

Freeze! Drop the cans and…Hey!!
I said freeze! Go, go! Get the…
Go, go! Radio back up! Go, go!

(pant)

        (pant)

                (pant)

Gotcha! Think it's funny?
To make us chase you?
Hey, no, no, no! Get
back here

(kick)

        (punch)

                (kick)   (punch)

I think this kid needs to relax
I think he needs help relaxing
Get your Taser out

Zzzzzzzap   Zzzzzzzap
Zzzzzzzap   Zzzzzzzap

(high fives)   (hooting)   (hollering)

Hey   He's not moving

2.

Red left your murdered heart
left the blood of every witness
Red cried *Fuck the flag!*
Red abandoned love
Red hated

Blue fell off veins
fell off police uniforms
Blue cried *Don't call me honor!*
Blue fled courage and crawled
back in the Krylon can you dropped

Yellow could only shine
like gold attracting greed
Yellow cried *Why death, today?*
Yellow stopped the dawn

Green remained green
soaked up every fallen thing
Green cried *Next time, always a next time*
Green changed all colors
Green waited for the rebirth

3.

Important things are invisible
Laws, promises, civil rights,
exist more in the ether
than on paper or in courts,
malleable and based solely
on discretion and hierarchy

What makes an American dream?
How does one become deserving?

Chorus

James Baldwin:

When you're writing

you're trying to find

something which you don't know

The angry Black man

in the room is

        invisible—

disarming, disengaging,
      not as dangerous
among the living as in
      the White   of imagination

      He be
Sanchez, Johnston, Harjo,
  Patel, and Shabazz,
he tip toe not tap dance,
mumble not mambo,
cry—not rain dance

Let's not simile, or
context the brotha, or—

let's just
piss him, poke him, push him

off
      Comportment Cliff,
music his meaning,
      funkify his fight

Knock, knock
Who's there?
Angry Black man
Angry Black man, who?

Me

Chorus

Miguel Piñero:

i dreamt i was this poeta
words glitterin' brite & bold

strikin' a new rush for gold
in las bodegas
where our poets' words & songs

are sung

Mamá Ana:

Write beautiful things, *Mijo,*

only beautiful things

black *Maybe*

The first friend I made in Elizabeth, New Jersey was a white kid named Billy. As a New York transplant my *Dominicano* look wasn't too popular with the Jersey folk. I had an Afro, wore dress pants, a collared shirt, and black leather shoes with little gold buckles. Most of the kids just wanted to know what my thing was. Billy and I couldn't have been more different, but we became close pretty quickly. Despite the fact that Billy's parents wouldn't allow him over my house, my grandmother would allow me over his. She took one look at Billy's blonde hair and blue eyes, and at his mother's middle class American manners, and pronounced their household safe. "Where are you from?" Billy's mother asked, referring to my grandmother's heavy accent. "I thought you were black." On that day I couldn't have imagined how many times I'd have to answer that question. "We're Dominican."

A couple years later, when the neighborhood became predominantly Cuban, African American and Haitian, Billy and his family moved away. My new best friend was black, and his mother wouldn't let him over my house either, on account of us being "Puerto Rican." You can imagine our surprise when I returned with a similar story. My grandmother didn't want me over his house because they were black. We looked each other over. Two skinny round headed, chocolate brown boys wondering what the hell each other's families were talking about. As far as we knew we looked the same. My grandmother was just as black as Tyshaun's mother and I told her as much every time she chided me about playing with him. What was I missing? My aunt took me to black barbershops for shape-ups and number ones. I spent a lot of time at Marvelous Marvin's crying as he picked my tender head before cutting it. Friends called me Del Monte because my head was so peasy. Yet my grandmother believed we were something other than what I was living, what I believed we were: black people who spoke Spanish. I was living a distorted Dominican version of Willie Perdomo's poem "Nigger-Reecan Blues:"

> —Hey, Willie. What are you, man? Boricua? Moreno? Que?
> Are you
> Black? Puerto Rican?
> —I am.
> —No, silly. You know what I mean: What are you?
> —I am you. You are me. We the same. Can't you feel our veins
> drinking the same blood?

56

—But who said you was a Porta-Reecan?
—Tu no eres Puerto Riqueño, brother.
—Maybe Indian like Gandhi-Indian?
—I thought you was a Black man.
—Is one of your parents white?
—You sure you ain't a mix of something like Cuban and Chinese?
—Looks like an Arab brother to me.
—Naahh, nah, nah. . .You ain't no Porty-Reecan.
—I keep tellin' y'all: That boy is a Black man with an accent.

As I got older I began to recognize the differences between African American culture, Afro-Latino culture, and being black in between. Black being the giant labels America puts on anyone darker than a paper bag. I also knew the word *Negro* well. I'd heard it my whole life in Spanish. What you mean when you say the word *Negro* depends heavily on the modifier because Latinos call each other *Negro* all the time: *Negrito lindo* (black and pretty), *mi Negro* (my black friend/brother), or *maldito Negro* (damned black guy). One thing remained steadfast: my family members never identified themselves as Africa black, and they never spoke about Dominican culture, or Dominican history, as having anything to do with Africa. The phrase *"Tu no eres negro,"* or *"No somos negro,"* was repeated over and over by my grand-uncles, and my grandmother. They'd use slurs like *cocolo*, and *monokiquillo* (basically monkey) when referring to African Americans or other people with strong African features. However, they referred to themselves and to me as *Indio*, a term which means of Indigenous descent. You could say I was more than a little confused growing up, but mostly I was angry. I knew what I saw in the mirror and what I experienced out in the world. Other Latinos repeatedly called me *cocolo*, and white cops called me *darkie* and *nigger*.

I felt like I was living in a perpetual *Twilight Zone* episode. I'm black in a country that by all indications hates black people, and I'm descended from people that are black, but pretend not to be black. Like most teenagers I was too wrapped up in it to see the bigger picture. There was some serious history behind all this un-blackness. And history starts at home.

*

My grandmother, Altagracia Felicia Garcia, was born in Santiago de los Caballeros, Dominican Republic, in 1933. She grew up during the height of Rafael Trujillo's dictatorship. Trujillo ruled the Dominican Republic for thirty years and his mania knew very little boundaries. He was a virulent racist and rapist. Trujillo ordered the deaths of countless Haitians and dark skinned Dominicans in a Hitler-style quest to "whiten" the Dominican Republic.

Snitches kept their ears open for three things: anybody disrespecting Trujillo or his regime, young beautiful girls for Trujillo to rape, and confirmation of Haitian blood in the family tree of Dominicans so they could be ripped out by the roots.

Julia Alvarez' novel *In the Time of the Butterflies*, and Junot Diaz' *The Brief Wondrous Life of Oscar Wao* depict snatches of daily life under the regime with particular accuracy. Dominicans living in this atmosphere were paranoid to put it mildly. Some wore makeup to make their complexions appear whiter; families hid their daughters and/or married them off and sent them to the mountains, or out of the country. People were given to spontaneously praising Trujillo in public so others could hear them.

I imagine my grandmother growing up in that country, staring in the mirror everyday, convincing herself she's not black/Haitian, and probably having to convince others. Maybe practicing the word *perejil* (parsley), even though she could roll her *r*'s perfectly, just in case she was put to the test. The French/Creole accent makes rolling the *r* in the Spanish word for parsley, *perejil,* difficult. The *r* sound comes out like a *th* or more commonly an *l* sound. In 1937, when my grandmother was four years old, Trujillo ordered that all the sugarcane plantation workers along the Dominican/Haitian border be given the parsley test, and those that couldn't pronounce the word were murdered in a massacre that killed thousands of Haitians and dark skinned Dominicans. Edwidge Danticat's novel *The Farming of Bones* is also a powerful and moving dramatization of the massacre, from the perspective of a young Haitian servant girl. Rita Dove also dramatized the Parsley Massacre of 1937 in her poem "Parsley."

El General has found his word: perejil.
Who says it, lives. He laughs, teeth shining
out of the swamp. The cane appears

in our dreams, lashed by wind and streaming.
And we lie down. For every drop of blood
there is a parrot imitating spring.
Out of the swamp the cane appears.

*

Dominican anti-blackness goes back even further than Trujillo's thirty-year reign of terror. During the colonial era, Spaniards set up a naming system called *las castas*, the word *casta* means caste. Under *las castas* Spaniards stood at the top of the social hierarchy, possessing all manner of wealth, power, and influence. As Spaniards copulated with the indigenous and African slave populations (by rape and sometimes, rarely, by marriage) their children were labeled and placed at a certain level within the hierarchy. For example, the child of an African and a Spaniard would be called a *Mulato*. The child of an African and a *Mulato* would be called a *Sambo*. The child of a Spaniard and an Indigenous person was called a *Mestizo*, and on and on. (It is important to note that these are zoological terms applicable to animals.) In order to move up in the social hierarchy everyone needed to be something else. The African or *Negro* wanted to pass as *mulato*, the *mulato* wanted to pass as Spaniard, or *Indio*, and nobody wanted to be *Negro*, black. Under *las castas* Africans were always at the bottom of the pyramid.

Trujillo built his sick twisted rule on top of *casta*. He took the manipulative colonial system of psychological conditioning and self-hate that Dominicans still internalized and magnified it with the power of ten thousand suns. In Trujillo's Dominican Republic denying blackness was life and death. I've heard people who grew up in communist countries tell their horror stories. Secret police picked up them or friends or family members because of an anonymous tip. They were tortured, imprisoned, or killed on the whispered word of some stranger. I think of the generations upon generations of Dominicans living that way, and how the racial/cultural mind fuck Trujillo created has been passed on in the island's DNA. I wonder how much of my grandmother's denial was a self-defense mechanism, how much was self-hate, and how much was just her carrying out what she was taught. After all those years, what did reality have to become.

My grandmother never spoke about her life during the Trujillo era. She owned a *colmado*, or a small grocery store in her village. I know this because when we lived in Harlem she also owned a *colmado* and she would say grocery stores were in her blood. When her Alzheimer's started, little bits of her past would come out unexpectedly, and finally my mother had to tell me the story. My grandmother escaped Dominican Republic after Trujillo was assassinated. Not only was she running from the burning shack, so to speak, she was also fleeing from an abusive husband. He was a tall, blond, honey colored man who owned lots of land, but was quick with his hands. Altagracia was not having that. She hustled her way to New York City carrying at least twenty years of "regime" in her veins, if not more.

*

In 1804, Haiti became the first colony to gain its independence, but independence came at a heavy price. The French repeatedly fought to retake the island, and ultimately forced the Haitian government to agree to a 150-million franc indemnity for the loss of lands and goods. The new Haitian government spread the ideals of freedom from slavery and tyranny. They aided South American revolutionary Simón Bolívar in his efforts to free Colombia and Venezuela from the Spaniards. When the Dominican Republic, then a Spanish colony called Santo Domingo, defeated Spanish colonialists in a revolt in 1821 they sought to unite the island under Haitian rule. For two decades Haiti and the Dominican Republic were one country, Spanish Haiti, but the economic yoke around Haiti's neck made sustained unification impossible. In 1844, in response to extreme taxation, Dominicans rebelled against the Haitians and established the Dominican Republic. You know the old saying; no good deed goes unpunished.

Since that time Haiti has struggled through some form or another of crushing international debt, economic stagnation, or government corruption. During Trujillo's rule all these different layers of history, colonialism, racism, massacres, corruption, and Haiti's perpetual economic hardships cemented a hate/hate relationship between the two countries.

*

As a child of Dominican immigrants I can say that my grandmother's people are suffering from serious ignorance. A kind of Stockholm syndrome, when a victim captured, abused, traumatized or beaten by a captor, begins to sympathize and empathize with that captor, exists within the Dominican Republic. They empathize; sympathize even, with *casta*, and the legacy of black hatred Trujillo left for them. Recently, the Dominican Republic's constitutional court passed a law stripping citizenship from thousands of Dominicans born of one or more Haitian parents. The spirit of the law seems to be geared towards deporting illegal Haitian immigrants, however, the fact is that for many born in poor rural and urban areas, documentation of births, deaths and when and where their ancestors entered the country is shaky at best.

Poverty and fear of deportation makes it difficult for Dominico-Haitians to prove their status. The situation is exacerbated by mob violence. Dominicans are roaming villages and cities, grabbing Haitians and dark-skinned Dominicans and brutalizing them. There has been at least one confirmed lynching. Bill Fletcher Jr. recently discussed this issue on his YouTube program The Global African. He noted that advocates of Dominico-Haitians are concerned because "it appears that the mechanism to identify possible deportees will be based off physical appearance. Specifically, dark skinned individuals."

I've read articles expressing outrage over what has been dubbed *La Sentencia*. Social media is buzzing with links, videos, and heated conversations. I also know that the United States has been conducting similar deportations. In fact, I'd be willing to wager that the Dominican constitutional court took their cue from us. Illegal immigrants and their children, children born and raised in America, have been deported back to their parents' country of origin. Some of these children don't even speak the language, usually Spanish. However, the US government has sent them packing, no questions asked, United States citizens. The *Huffington Post* reports that, "When a parent is deported, their U.S.-born children sometimes leave with them. But some stay in the U.S. with another parent or family member. Some children end up in U.S. foster care." In 2013, more than 72,000 illegal immigrants with American-born children were deported.

It used to be that if you were an illegal immigrant and your child was born in this country, you were given legal residency, and you were given a green card. That doesn't appear to be the case any longer.

*

Here's some hard shit for people to deal with, especially Latinos. I love *bachata*, *salsa*, *merengue*, rice and beans. I grew up watching annual reruns of *Roots*, every episode of *Diff'rent Strokes*, dancing along with Michael Jackson, rapping Public Enemy's lyrics, and I rocked a Gumby and a high top fade when that was the style. None of these loves was or is mutually exclusive of the others. Growing up I identified (and still do) with black culture, arts, music, fashion, everything, because that's what we looked like, what we are, not African American, but black.

This is not to say that there's some formulaic definition of blackness, or what Amiri Baraka called "a static cultural essence to blacks." There is not. Neither is blackness that marketable, sellable product or anger Claudia Rankine criticizes Hennessy Youngman for pushing, in chapter two of *Citizen: An American Lyric*:

> On the bridge between this sellable anger and "the artist" resides, at times, an actual anger. Youngman in his video doesn't address this type of anger: the anger built up through experience and the quotidian struggles against dehumanization every brown or black person lives simply because of skin color.

God forbid blackness should ever be described as Rachel Dolezal. Instead, I think of Aimé Césaire's *Négritude* "…the awareness of being black, the simple acknowledgment of a fact which implies the acceptance of it, a taking charge of one's destiny as a black man [person], of one's history and culture." We must take Négritude beyond the borders of literary movements and make "taking charge" part of our very fabric.

In high school I rarely got along with the Dominicans that had just arrived to America. They watched me suspiciously, my slang, my easygoing nature with black, white, gay, and straight. The fact that my best friend was black, and that the rest of my crew consisted of Cuban, Colombian, Puerto Rican, Filipino, and Ecuadorian, was a big bone of contention for the new arrivals. Something about the way I carried myself troubled my *paisanos* and there was no going back. I was called a fake Dominican on several occasions, and I relished the role of outcast. My motto was "fuck your racist bullshit. You don't even know your history."

Perhaps they didn't yet understand that America thrusts black or white upon you quickly, you have to decide, you have to know who and what you are. Life in Dominican Republic had been too culturally ignorant and insular. Meanwhile in America, some euro-centric or Castilian Latinos are passing for white, but Afro-Latinos are either self-hating or catching hell or both, or just plain confused about who the hell they are. Most of the Dominicans I know have a discernable African lineage, but too many are quick to claim Latin American status as opposed to Afro-Caribbean identity. Let's be honest, Cuba, Puerto Rico, Dominican Republic, and Haiti aren't in South or Central America, they're in the Caribbean. We need to re-examine our historical cultural selves. I completely agree that race is a construct, but identity is a necessity.

I've met a lot of European immigrants in America, both first and second generation. They come to America and assimilate quickly into white culture. The children of African diaspora, for complex reasons, have some difficulty owning our blackness. Yes, history has a lot to do with it; what our families teach us also has a lot to do with it. We must overcome these factors, educate ourselves, and become a part of the larger conversation, the critical one about how much Black Lives Matter. They're killing us out here, and in places like the Dominican Republic, we're killing each other.

*

In his essay "Encounter on the Seine: Black Meets Brown," James Baldwin explores differences between the American children of African diaspora and their colonial cousins; Antiguans, Martiniquais, and St. Lucians, just to name a few. Perhaps the most critical peculiarity Baldwin observes is the African American disconnect from a black nation, the loss of black hegemony, and the resulting psychological trauma.

The African before him has endured privation, injustice,
medieval cruelty; but the African has not yet endured the
utter alienation of himself from his people and his past…and
he has not, all his life long, ached for acceptance in a culture
which pronounced straight hair and white skin the only
acceptable beauty (38).

Isn't this a derivative of the Haitian/Dominican struggle? Haiti is strongly
tethered to its past, to its identity as a nation comprised of children from
Africa, while the Dominican Republic is trying to be anything but. The
Dominican idea of identity and beauty and acceptance is rooted in euro-
centric ideas of beauty.

My grandmother, our extended family, and Dominicans I know have
taught me that changing hearts and minds is difficult work. It takes time,
but it also requires revelatory experiences, and forging new memories that
can smooth the scar tissue of old traumas. Unfortunately, Haitians and
their Dominican-born children don't have that kind of time. My individual
effort at accepting my blackness, my history, and my attempt to build a
way forward isn't helping them.

But America and the Civil Rights movement have taught me that I
have options. I can exercise my political power by writing a petition asking
the President of the United States to pressure the Dominican government
to ensure that the rights of Dominicans born of Haitian descent are
protected. And that Haitians facing legal deportation are not butchered
or beaten in the streets. This petition should demand that our President
threaten to cut off aid and issue sanctions if the Dominican Republic does
not comply. I can reach out to my local and state representatives and ask
them to support the petition. I can use my social media presence and
challenge friends, family, and celebrities to put their names behind it.

Just as importantly, I can tell my story, the truths I've pieced together
from history's lies. If you're white, take what you've learned from this
essay and put your privilege to work. I don't mean that disrespectfully,
honestly. If you're like me, black, Dominican, American, and you love
your Dominican grandmother or mother, even though they talk that shit
you can't wrap your head around, seek the knowledge and then educate
them, whether they like it or not. Start the process of figuring out how the
Dominican American experience can help island Dominicans get their lives
together. Start the conversations that can actively inform the Afro-Latino
experience and the Afro-Caribbean identity. How does the Afro-Latino/
Caribbean experience in America mirror the African American experience
for you? We need to talk about this. In time, these conversations can help

all Dominicans to be more like our Haitian brothers and sisters, proud to walk black and beautiful in the sun.

Sources

Home [An Irrevocable Condition]

Criss, Anthony, and Vincent Brown. *Uptown Anthem*. Naughty by Nature. DJ Kay Gee, 1991. Vinyl recording.

Rukeyser, Muriel. "The Poem as Mask" *Muriel Rukeyser: Selected Poems*. Ed. Adrienne Cecile Rich. New York: Library of America, 2004. N. pag. Print.

Carter, Sean. By Kanye West, M. Price, and D. Walsh. *Heart of the City (Ain't No Love)*. Jay-Z. Kanye West, 2001. Vinyl recording.

Def, Mos. Hip Hop. Mos Def. Diamond D, Mos Def, 1999. Vinyl recording.

black *Maybe*:

Altman, Susan. "Haiti, Republic of." *Encyclopedia of African-American Heritage. New York: Facts On File, 2000*. History Research Center. Web. 2 Aug. 2015.

Baldwin, James. "Encounter on the Seine: Black Meets Brown." *The Price of the Ticket: Collected Nonfiction, 1948-1985*. New York: St Martin's, 1985. 35-39. Print.

Foley, Elise. "Deportation Separated Thousands Of U.S.-Born Children From Parents In 2013." *TheHuffingtonPost.com*, 25 June 2014. Web. 12 July 2015.

Perdomo, Willie. "Nigger-Reecan Blues." *Where a Nickel Costs a Dime*. New York: W.W. Norton, 1996. 19-21. Print.

Rankine, Claudia. "II." *Citizen: An American Lyric*. Minneapolis: Graywolf, 2014. 23-24. Print.

"The Global African: Hostility in the D.R.,Verizon, Football." YouTube. Bill Fletcher Jr., 29 June 2015. Web. 12 July 2015.

Resources

Thomas, Piri. *Down These Mean Streets*. New York: Vintage, NY. Print.

Quiñonez, Ernesto. *Bodega Dreams*. New York: Vintage Contemporaries, 2000. Print.

Baraka, Amiri. *Tales of the Out & the Gone*. New York: Akashic, 2007. Print.

Baraka, Amiri. *Preface to a Twenty Volume Suicide Note ....* New York: Totem, 1961. Print.

Baldwin, James. *Notes of a Native Son*. London: Michael Joseph, 1964. Print.

Piñero, Miguel. *La Bodega Sold Dreams*. Houston, TX: Arte Público, 1980. Print.

Reiter, Bernd, and Kimberly Eison. Simmons. *Afro-descendants, Identity, and the Struggle for Development in the Americas*. East Lansing: Michigan State UP, 2012. Print.

Perdomo, Willie. *Where a Nickel Costs a Dime*. New York: W.W. Norton, 1996. Print.

Perdomo, Willie. *Smoking Lovely*. New York, NY: Rattapallax, 2003. Print.

Ellis, Thomas Sayers. *Skin, Inc.: Identity Repair Poems*. Minneapolis, MN: Graywolf, 2010. Print.

Rankine, Claudia. *Citizen: An American Lyric*. Minnesota: Graywolf, 2014. Print.

Candelario, Ginetta E. B. *Black Behind the Ears: Dominican Racial Identity from Museums to Beauty Shops*. Durham: Duke University Press, 2007. Print.

Thanks & Praise

Bismillāhi raḥmāni raḥīm — All gratitude & reverence to the Almighty God, The Most Gracious, The Most Merciful.

Thanks and praise to Aracelis Girmay, for your friendship, for all the pivotal questions, the insightful and necessary conversations, and the generous and patient reading and re-reading of the manuscript. Mad love.

Thanks and praise to Alicia Ostriker, for calling bullshit when it needed to be called and for encouraging the ambition and vision I had when I started this book, before I knew what it would become. Mad love.

Thanks and praise to Ann Davenport, for your brilliant editorial eye and nitpickiness, and for your generosity with your gifts. Mad love.

Thanks and praise to all the men, women, and children who died and fought in the struggle against the human construction that is racism, and to those who continue to fight and sacrifice and die.

Thanks and praise to Randall Horton and Heather Buchanan and Willow, for believing in this book when so many others didn't. Mad love.

Thanks and praise to my family, to Ana Felicia Garcia de Rodriguez, to Altagracia Felicia Garcia, to Kyana Melissa Garcia — forever in my heart, in my dreams, in my memories.

And to Dominicans everywhere, we gonna get our shit together, coño. Mad love.

About the Author

Roberto Carlos Garcia's book, *Melancolía*, is available from Červená Barva Press. *black / Maybe* is his second collection. Roberto's poems and prose have appeared or are forthcoming in *The Root, Those People, Rigorous, Academy of American Poets Poem-A-Day, The New Engagement, Public Pool, Stillwater Review, Gawker, Barrelhouse, Tuesday; An Art Project, The Acentos Review, Lunch Ticket*, and many others.

He is the founder of the cooperative press Get Fresh Books, LLC.

A native New Yorker, Roberto holds an MFA in Poetry and Poetry in Translation from Drew University and has been nominated for a Pushcart Prize.

His website is http://www. robertocarlosgarcia.com/

9 780999 223291

CPSIA info
at www.IC
Printed in t
BVRC0921
627100BV